TAPAS

NEW
HOLLAND

Tapas

TOMAS GARCIA

First published in 2006 by
New Holland Publishers (UK) Ltd
London • Cape Town • Sydney • Auckland
Text and photographs copyright © 2005
New Holland Publishers (UK) Ltd
Copyright © 2006 New Holland Publishers (UK) Ltd

Garfield House
86–88 Edgware Road
London W2 2EA
www.newhollandpublishers.com

Unit 1, 66 Gibbes Street
Chatswood
NSW 2067
Australia

80 McKenzie Street
Cape Town 8001
South Africa

218 Lake Road
Northcote
Auckland
New Zealand

ISBN 978 1 84537 628 4

SENIOR EDITOR: Corinne Masciocchi
DESIGN CONCEPT: Christelle Marais
DESIGNER: Rod Teasdale
PHOTOGRAPHY: Stuart West
FOOD STYLING: Stella Murphy
PRODUCTION: Marion Storz
EDITORIAL DIRECTION: Rosemary Wilkinson

Reproduction by Pica Digital PTE Ltd, Singapore
Printed and bound by Tien Wah Press, Malaysia

3 5 7 9 10 8 6 4 2

CONTENTS

INTRODUCTION

It could be argued that Spain has the most civilized bar culture in the world. Tapas are fundamental to this way of life. They are those delicious morsels that appear magically next to that drink you've just ordered in any number of bars, from San Sebastian in the north, across to Santiago in the northwest, through Madrid to Barcelona in the east and down to Seville and Granada, the Moorish south.

Spanish bars are, before anything else, welcoming. Their sophistication lies in their ability to produce and serve an entire range, from soothing comfort food to exacting haute cuisine. The local in Spain is a bar where you can have a quick breakfast on the way to work, or a couple of drinks with friends on your way home. It is where everyone, from great-grandma to the squirming infant, can enjoy a drink and some food, usually to

socialize before lunch or dinner. This is family life conducted at large. The huge variety of tapas dishes means there is always something for everyone and they have a mellowing effect on those consuming alcohol – ultimately this means that the atmosphere is more relaxed and gregarious.

This book aims to introduce you to tapas you can make with confidence at home. Authentic Spanish ingredients are now available around the world, not only in specialist delicatessens, but also in ordinary supermarkets. The Spanish themselves are responding to the global village by using a much wider range of ingredients. Soy and Worcester sauces, papaya and avocado, smoked salmon, curry paste – even Maldon salt are

commonplace, casually but tellingly incorporated to satisfy ever more sophisticated palates.

Spanish cooking is a rich and identifiable tradition which proudly reflects its regionalism. For every pan-Iberian staple such as the tortilla, or potato omelette, there are a dozen dishes particular to a locality. The variations are subtle and are the result of differing local ingredients. This book aims to reflect the typically Spanish as well as the new developments in creative tapas increasingly surfacing in modern bars. The only criteria worth acknowledging are: does it satisfy your appetite? Does it enhance and complement that drink that has delicately teased those gastric juices? With this book, I hope the answer will be yes.

HISTORY
OF TAPAS

There are many theories as to the origin of tapas. Some say that this culinary tradition was invented by Alfonso X, known as the Wise, King of Castille and Leon – or rather by his chef, who treated the King's exhaustion with a daily succession of very small dishes, each helped along with a small glass of wine. His recovery was so remarkable that the old king tried to spread the news: eat little and often, he commanded, and you will live longer.

A less charming explanation for the origin of tapas is the Spanish verb *tapar*, meaning 'to cover'. Slices of ham or cheese were used to cover the *potes*, clay wine cups, ostensibly to keep out the flies. From these scarcely hygienic beginnings was elaborated the wondrous range of tapas we know today. Another theory is that they developed as a way of boosting energy in the middle of the day, or as a post-siesta pick-me-up.

Gradually it became clear that tapas were not only delicious and satisfying to consume but were also useful to the body in that they soaked up some of the accompanying alcohol. Olives and nuts or slices of sausage, both *salchichón* and *chorizo* styles, fish freshly fried or preserved in oil or pickled in vinegar, fried dough with all manner of flavourings, all became staples. The New World offered up its bounty, with the humble potato

outstandingly affording a range of possibilities, not least of which is the always welcome potato omelette, the *tortilla*.

And it is a living tradition, reflecting the changing world, as new ingredients and small but perfectly formed fantasies are plated up before the feasting eyes and rumbling appetites of devotees. The tapa tradition, the Spaniard's drink and a bite in his local, is stronger than ever.

HOW TO
SERVE TAPAS

Tapas is a general term for small snacks, defined best by being eaten comfortably standing up to accompany your drink. They come in a variety of different forms and can be anything from a handful of stuffed olives to a crisp deep-fried artichoke to a gently simmering chorizo stew. The recipes in this book are divided up according to how they would be served in a Spanish bar. Cocktail sticks are an essential tool in the enjoyment of tapas and are used to spear or pierce a whole range of tapas. In Spain these are known as *pinchos*, from the verb *pinchar*, meaning to prick or pierce. *Pinchos* have come to mean any tapas that are served on or with cocktail sticks and skewers. There is a whole range of tapas that are arranged in layers on toasted bread, rather like the Italian *crostini*: in Spain they are called montados or tostas, which is a better explanation of what they are. Pastry tartlets become useful 'containers' – all manner of delicious ingredients can be piled into a puff pastry tart.

The joy of tapas, for most people, is that they can enjoy three or four different dishes without feeling that they are overeating. When preparing tapas, it is a good idea to create a balance of dishes and to choose items that complement and contrast with one another. Think about the sharp tang of a dish of marinated anchovies, the paprika-flavoured spicy chorizo or the robust flavour of a garlicky pork brochette – and work out how well these dishes work together. If you are catering for a party, don't make things too complicated for yourself and just concentrate on a few dishes. Some tapas, such as the *gildas* can be prepared in advance.

Tapas were developed to complement wine but they can of course be enjoyed with other drinks. Today, it is a safe bet to say that more beer than wine is drunk in Spanish bars, especially amongst younger people. In many bars you will find that it is common practice to ask for a *corto*, a wine glass of beer to drink with your tapa. Smaller drinks work better because of the habit of moving from bar to bar, variously called the *tapeo* or *chiquiteo*. It is a triumph of evolved social engineering: the proportion of food to alcohol is friendlier, people move around a small area full of small bars and inevitably run into familiar faces, and a large number of smaller bars are guaranteed custom, able to offer a wide or specialised range of fresh tapas cheaply to conveyor loads of customers. Instant, fluent conviviality.

Tapas also go ideally with sherry. Jerez de la Frontera and Sanlúcar de Barrameda both produce excellent wines whose nobility has been favourably compared with those of Champagne. A chilled fino, oloroso or manzanilla is a perfect accompaniment to the food in this book.

INGREDIENTS

Although we have become used to an ever wider selection of ingredients from around the world in our supermarkets, authentic Spanish tapas are today still based on the traditional range of ingredients that have evolved over the centuries. These are the staples which should be your starting point when planning a tapas menu at home.

Most simple of all is a handful of olives, available in the most rudimentary of bars, if only directly from a tin onto a saucer. You can do much better: olives stuffed with anchovies, pimentos, almonds, lemon, for instance, as well a wide selection of different olives in herbs, garlic, lemon and so on.

The two other ingredients of the classic tapa *gilda* are widely available and easily stored. The *guindilla* is a small hot chilli in vinegar and the *boqueron* is the silvery anchovy preserved in oil

and vinegar, giving it a characteristically delicate flavour, quite unlike the more familiar dark salted variety.

Spaniards are justly proud of their cured ham, *jamón*. The best quality is *jamón ibérico*, made from giant black pigs that traditionally graze on acorns in the extensive oak forests of Extremadura in the western area of Spain. Otherwise, you will now see *jamón serrano*, cured in exactly the same way and exported worldwide, in your local supermarkets. The Spanish do like to serve it thicker cut than the paper-thin Parma of the Italians – a matter of taste.

There are many varieties of the chorizo, such as the magnificent mature *ibérico* version that can be sliced thick or thin, or the less cured smaller versions used for cooking, either to enliven stews and pulses or roasted in wine, crunchy and juicy.

Pimientos de piquillo are an object lesson in how a high quality ingredient can be made widely available. They are small red peppers or pimentos, char-grilled and peeled, and then marinated. This process brings out a magnificent sweet, tangy flavour, a superb complementary ingredient in many Spanish dishes.

There can be no real taste of Mediterranean cooking without olive oil. Like the grape, the apparently humble olive responds to the soil and climate it's grown in to give subtly varying, characteristic tastes, hardly any two oils identical in flavour. It is entirely possible to have a range of olive oils to hand which will fill your every need, satisfy your every culinary desire. Extra-virgin olive oil is used for dressings, its strong, fruity flavour the result of a first, cold pressing. It is justifiably expensive and its low burning threshold makes it unsuitable for hot frying. Virgin olive oil is almost always good enough for dressings, usually has a less intense flavour and can be used for hot frying. A third type, often labelled 'pomace' olive oil, is pressed from the skin and stone of the olive after the first pressings. It can be very cheap and yet it still retains a very good flavour. Its high burning threshold makes it ideal for frying.

The spice most prevalent in Spanish cuisine is *pimentón*, which we know as paprika. This is dried and powdered red pimento and is available as *pimentón picante* (hot) or *pimentón dulce* (mild). In some cases it may even be smoked. It's what gives chorizo its unmistakeable taste.

No Spanish kitchen can function without garlic and its classic combination with parsley, salt and olive oil, what the French call a *persillade*, is used as a marinade, the basis for a sauce with meat or fish, or as a simple condiment for added flavour.

The Spanish love seafood and they have a huge variety of it pickled, sauced, soused, generally preserved in cans or jars. They are staples in supermarkets and are becoming more widely available outside Spain. These are so tasty, so intensely flavoured that all you need do is serve them on a tosta. *Mejillones en escabeche* (marinated mussels) are available tinned, as well as squid, octopus, clams, cockles, the humble sardine and yet more obscure molluscs. They all positively improve by being cooked and thus preserved.

Many of the recipes in this book call for prawns – I would always recommend going to your local fishmonger and buying fresh prawns, preferably with tail on. Alternatively, frozen prawns also work well and will defrost in no time.

Bacalao is an important Spanish ingredient but is not as widespread outside of Spain. There are many perfectly good alternatives, such as good, undyed smoked haddock, however, if you can get hold of it, it is worth the effort. *Bacalao* is effectively cod which has been preserved by being salted and dried. The success of salt cod depends very much on the quality of the fish more than anything else. Try to avoid buying thin, meagre pieces: the plumper the better. Before using, it needs thorough desalination – you must use plenty of water and allow at least 24 hours. Soak in clean, fresh water and change the water about three or four times, then drain and pat the piece dry. You should be able to skin the fish quite easily and there will be bones to pick out (use tweezers to remove the tiniest of these).

STORE CUPBOARD

Here you will find a list of ingredients you should have in your kitchen. Together with the fresh ingredients necessary for a particular tapa, this selection will enable you to prepare everything you will find to tempt you in this book.

KITCHEN SHELF

- ❖ Fresh garlic
- ❖ Parsley plant
- ❖ Coriander plant
- ❖ Free-range eggs

FRIDGE

- ❖ Lemons
- ❖ Limes
- ❖ Unsalted butter
- ❖ Streaky bacon or *pancetta*
- ❖ *Jamón serrano*

FREEZER

- ❖ Frozen peas (petits pois have more flavour)
- ❖ Frozen spinach
- ❖ Packets of vol-au-vent cases
- ❖ Ready-made puff-pastry
- ❖ Good-quality sea salt
- ❖ Jars of marinated seafood
- ❖ English mustard powder
- ❖ Extra-virgin olive oil
- ❖ Light olive oil
- ❖ Sherry vinegar

LARDER

- Tinned tuna
- Tinned tomatoes
- Tinned petits pois
- Tinned artichoke hearts
- Tinned chickpeas
- Green olives, pitted and/or stuffed with anchovies, *pimientos*, lemon etc.
- Tins or jars of *pimientos de piquillo* (chargrilled ones have a better flavour)
- Jars of *guindilla* chillies (small hot green chillies in vinegar)
- Mild smoked paprika (*pimentón dulce*)
- Hot smoked paprika (*pimentón picante*), chilli powder or cayenne pepper
- Jars of tapenade (black olive paste)
- Curry paste
- Ground turmeric
- Ground cumin
- Ground coriander
- Brandy or *orujo*, the equivalent of the French *marc* or Italian *grappa*, a very dry, clear eau-de-vie

EQUIPMENT

As this is a book about preparing tapas in the comfort of your home, it follows that you are not going to need a lot of professional catering equipment to prepare them. However, a few basic items, most of which you will probably already have, will help make preparing these dishes as quick and as stress-free as possible.

Knives and boards

This is your preparation world in microcosm. Add only a source of heat, and you could say all the basic equipment needs are satisfied. People can be very intense about kitchen knives – and are prepared to pay a premium to give themselves an edge (so to speak!) Good, sharp knives are important, but you do not have to pay through the nose for them. You'll manage with one small and one large knife for chopping, and a steel or carborundum block to keep them sharp. It's not helpful to chuck them into a drawer after use, as this exposure dulls the blade, so a block or a sheath is recommended. A third knife, with a serrated edge, is good for slicing softer items, such as tomatoes. A good chopping board is essential, so choose one that you feel at home with. I find wooden boards more satisfying than cold, efficient plastic. Try to keep different boards for different jobs, as a wooden board will often retain the smell of garlic and onions.

Frying pans

The preference for fried food in Spain is reflected in a number of the recipes in this book. At least two good frying pans are necessary. Good-quality non-stick are essential, unless you have cast-iron skillets which need seasoning.

Saucepans

Stainless steel heavy-based saucepans are excellent, but aluminium pans with a heavy, heat-conducting base are perfectly fine. A small, spouted, heavy milk pan is also useful.

Food processor and blender

For the purposes of these recipes, no electric appliance is really necessary. But with the help of a food processor or blender, certain otherwise tedious and time-consuming jobs are made much easier and speedier, such as chopping large quantities of herbs, making mayonnaise or aïoli, or mincing meat.

Other equipment

Make sure you have a selection of wooden spoons, a palette knife, a slotted spoon, a grater, heatproof tongs, a vegetable peeler, various bowls, kitchen foil and baking parchment to hand. A good store of basic kitchen utensils and materials will make preparing the recipes in this book an effortless pleasure. Cocktail sticks, wooden skewers and a variety of small serving plates and bowls are essential for serving up your tapas.

Egg and cheese

Simple yet deliciously mouthwatering recipes using favourite tapas ingredients.

Revuelto de esparragos trigueros

Scrambled eggs with asparagus

Makes 10–12 toasts

1 French stick, cut into 1-cm (½-in) rounds
Olive oil for brushing
225 g (8 oz) thin asparagus
4 eggs, beaten
Salt and freshly ground black pepper
1 Tbsp good-quality olive oil or 1 oz (25 g) butter
1–2 Tbsp grated hard cheese, such as Parmesan or Manchego (optional)

Preheat the oven to 190°C (375°F/Gas Mark 5). Brush the bread with a little oil, place on a baking tray and bake for 5 minutes or until golden brown. Cut the asparagus into three pieces and drop into a pan of boiling, salted water. Bring back to the boil and simmer for no longer than 1 minute, less if the asparagus is really thin. Remove from the pan and refresh under cold running water.

Add the asparagus to the beaten eggs and season well. Heat the oil or butter in a medium frying pan. Add the egg and asparagus mixture to the pan and cook gently, stirring frequently. As the eggs set, sprinkle on the cheese, if using. Spoon the mixture onto the toasts and serve immediately.

Tomates rellenos de huevos

Egg mayonnaise tomatoes

Makes 12

12 small tomatoes
4 eggs
2 Tbsp mayonnaise
2 Tbsp chopped spring onions or cress
Salt and freshly ground black pepper
1 tsp paprika

Remove the stalks then slice off and reserve the top of each tomato. Scoop out and discard the seeds to make room for the stuffing.

Place the eggs in a medium pan, cover withcold water and bring to the boil, then simmer for a further 2 to 3 minutes. Allow to cool in cold water. Peel the eggs and dice into fine cubes. Add the mayonnaise and spring onions and season well. Fill the tomatoes with the mixture to overflowing, sprinkle with paprika and cap with the reserved tops, if you wish.

Croquetas de huevos
Egg croquettes

Makes about 36

100 g (3½ oz) butter
125 g (4½ oz) plain flour
250 ml (9 fl oz) cold milk
2 hard-boiled eggs, finely chopped
Salt and freshly ground black pepper
1 tsp grated nutmeg
5 or 6 Tbsp fine breadcrumbs
2 large eggs, beaten
Oil for deep-frying

Melt the butter in a medium saucepan and add the flour, stirring continuously. Allow the flour to cook in the butter for a couple of minutes, stirring continuously. Add the cold milk little by little, stirring all the while until you have a thick, smooth sauce. Fold in the finely chopped hard-boiled eggs, season well and add the nutmeg. Continue to cook for 4 to 5 minutes. The end result should be quite thick. It is essential that the mixture is allowed to cool completely – overnight is best.

Take a scant tablespoon of the mixture and form into a croquette, a 3–4 cm (1½–2 in) cylinder. Roll the croquette in the breadcrumbs, then coat in the beaten egg and roll in the breadcrumbs again. Make sure the breadcrumbs are always dry to ensure an even coating.

Heat the oil in a large, heavy-based pan until the temperature reaches 180°C (350°F). Fry in batches of no more than 3 or 4 for about 5 minutes until golden brown. Remove with a slatted spoon, drain on kitchen paper and serve immediately.

Aïoli
Garlic mayonnaise

Serves 10

2 large egg yolks
3 cloves garlic, peeled and crushed
2 tsp vinegar or lemon juice
Pinch of English mustard powder (optional)
Salt and freshly ground black pepper
350 ml (12 fl oz) light olive oil
2 Tbsp warm water

Put the egg yolks, garlic, vinegar or lemon juice, mustard, if using, salt and pepper in a blender or food processor and whizz briefly. With the motor running, very slowly trickle in the oil until the mixture thickens and emulsifies. Add the water at the end.

Aïoli is delicious slathered on roasted new potatoes or as a dip for fried potato wedges.

Aïoli estragon
Tarragon aïoli

Serves 10

2 large egg yolks
2 tsp vinegar or lemon juice
Pinch of English mustard powder (optional)
Salt and freshly ground black pepper
350 ml (12 fl oz) light olive oil
2 Tbsp warm water
1 Tbsp chopped fresh tarragon

Put the egg yolks, vinegar or lemon juice, mustard, if using, salt and pepper in a blender or food processor and whizz briefly. With the motor running, very slowly trickle in the oil until the mixture thickens and emulsifies. Add the water at the end and stir in the chopped fresh tarragon.

Tarragon aïoli is delicious on roasted new potatoes or as a dip for fried potato wedges.

Tortilla flamenca
Flamenco omelette

Makes 24 pinchos

2 Tbsp oil
225 g (8 oz) onions, peeled and diced
200 g (7 oz) mushrooms, sliced
200 g (7 oz) ham, cut into 5-cm (2-in) strips
225 g (8 oz) tinned red pimentos, drained weight, cut into strips
225 g (8 oz) petits pois, thawed if frozen
Salt and freshly ground black pepper
6 large eggs, beaten
1 large clove garlic, peeled and crushed

Soften the onions in the oil for 3 to 4 minutes, add the mushrooms and cook for a further 5 minutes. Add the ham strips, stir and cook for 1 minute, before adding the pimento strips. Finally add the petits pois, stir and heat through for 1 minute. Season. Pour the mixture into the eggs, along with the crushed garlic.

Return the pan to the heat and add just enough oil to cover the base in a thin film. Add the egg, onion and mushroom mixture, spreading it evenly around the pan. Cook over a high heat for about 2 minutes, being careful not to allow it to stick to the bottom. Remove from the heat.

Oil a plate and place it over the frying pan, then carefully invert the pan to reveal a golden brown omelette. Return the pan to the heat, adding a teaspoon of oil. Slide the tortilla off the plate and into the pan. Cook for a further 1 to 2 minutes. Turn out on to the plate. The golden brown tortilla should be set, yet still soft in the centre. Cut into eight segments, then cut each segment into three and serve.

Queso de cabra con salsa picante

Goat's cheese with chilli sauce

Makes 24 pinchos

340 g (12 oz) firm goat's cheese
4–5 chillies, deseeded and diced
250 ml (9 fl oz) olive oil
Salt and freshly ground black pepper
Juice of ½ lemon

Cut the cheese into 2-cm (¾-in) cubes. In a bowl, mix the chillies with the oil and season with salt and pepper. Add the cubes of cheese to the oil and mix well. Allow to marinate for a couple of hours. Squeeze the lemon over the cheese and mix again. Serve on cocktail sticks.

Croquetas de queso
Cheese croquettes

Makes 24

900 g (2 lb) floury potatoes, e.g. King Edward
50 g (2 oz) butter
2 eggs, beaten
75 g (2½ oz) grated hard cheese, such as Parmesan or
Manchego or 50 g (2 oz) crumbled blue cheese,
such as Roquefort or Cabrales
Salt and freshly ground black pepper
1 tsp grated nutmeg
1 tsp mustard powder
2 Tbsp chopped parsley
1–2 Tbsp seasoned flour
2 large eggs, beaten
2–3 Tbsp fine breadcrumbs
350 ml (12 fl oz) oil for deep-frying

Boil the potatoes, then drain and mash with the butter.
Fold in the eggs and cheese. Season with salt and pepper,
adding the nutmeg, mustard powder and parsley. This
mixture should be firm but not overly smooth. Allow
to cool.

Take a scant tablespoon of the mixture and form into a
croquette, a 3–4 cm (1½–2 in) cylinder. Roll the croquette
in the flour then coat in the beaten egg and roll in the
breadcrumbs.

Heat the oil in a large, heavy-based pan until the temperature reaches 180°C (350°F). Fry in batches of no more than 3 or 4 for about 5 minutes until golden brown. Remove with a slatted spoon, drain on kitchen paper and serve immediately.

Huevos rellenos con alcaparras
Eggs stuffed with capers and gherkins

Makes 24

12 small eggs
6 Tbsp mayonnaise
1 tsp mustard
Salt and freshly ground black pepper
1 Tbsp chopped capers
1 Tbsp chopped gherkins

Hard-boil the eggs, peel and cut in half lengthways. Scoop out the yolks and mash them together with the mayonnaise and mustard. Season well. Add the capers and gherkins to the mayonnaise mixture, heap back into the egg halves and serve.

Huevos rellenos de bonito

Tuna-stuffed eggs

Makes 24

12 small eggs
6 Tbsp mayonnaise
1 tsp mustard
Salt and freshly ground black pepper
185-g (6½-oz) tin good-quality tuna
Fresh parsley, to garnish

Hard-boil the eggs, peel and cut in half lengthways. Scoop out the yolks and mash them together with the mayonnaise and mustard. Season well. Drain the tuna and flake. Add it to the mayonnaise mixture and heap the mixture back into the egg halves. Serve garnished with parsley.

Tortilla de espinacas
Spinach and cheese tortilla

Makes 24 pinchos

450 g (1 lb) potatoes, peeled and cubed
225 g (8 oz) onions, peeled and diced
350 ml (12 fl oz) oil for frying
Salt and freshly ground black pepper
3 large eggs
1 large clove garlic, peeled and crushed
225 g (8 oz) spinach, drained weight (freshly wilted)
225 g (8 oz) grated Cheddar, Gruyère,
Parmesan or Manchego cheese
Pinch of grated nutmeg

Mix the potatoes and onions together in a bowl. Heat the oil in a medium-size non-stick frying pan, add the potato and onion mixture then turn down the heat slightly. Season with salt and pepper and stir the mixture regularly, so that it does not stick to the bottom, for 10 minutes or until the potato is cooked. Turn the mixture out into a strainer over a bowl and reserve the oil.

Beat the eggs in a large bowl and whisk in the crushed garlic. Fold the spinach and the grated cheese into the egg mixture along with the nutmeg. Add the egg mixture to potatoes and onions and mix thoroughly.

Return the pan to the heat and add just enough of the oil to cover the base in a thin film. Add the egg and potato mixture, spreading it evenly around the pan. Cook over a high heat for about 2 minutes, being careful not to allow it to stick to the bottom. Remove from the heat.

Oil a plate and place it over the frying pan, then carefully invert the pan to reveal a golden brown omelette. Return the pan to the heat, adding a teaspoon of the oil. Slide the tortilla off the plate and into the pan. Cook for a further 1 to 2 minutes. Turn out on to the plate. The golden brown tortilla should be set, yet still soft in the centre and the potatoes crumbly. Cut into eight segments, then cut each segment into three and serve.

Queso de burgos
Chicory cheese boats

Makes 8–10

1 medium head chicory
225 g (8 oz) queso de burgos or mozzarella
3 pimientos de piquillo (see page 23)
12 good-quality, pink anchovy fillets
Salt and freshly ground black pepper
1 tsp paprika

Cut the end off the endive and loosen the leaves to make the 'boats' for the cheese. Rinse the leaves and pat dry.

Cut the cheese and pimientos into strips the width of the anchovies. Mix the three ingredients together with a little of the oil from the jar of anchovies. Season with pepper and a little salt. Load the endive leaves with the mixture and sprinkle with paprika.

Tortilla de ajos tiernos
Spring garlic tortilla

Makes 8–10 toasts

1 French stick, cut into 1-cm (½-in) rounds
Olive oil, for brushing
225 g (8 oz) spring garlic or spring onions
1 Tbsp good-quality olive oil or 25 g (1 oz) butter
4 eggs, beaten
Salt and freshly ground black pepper

Preheat the oven to 190°C (375°F/Gas Mark 5). Brush the bread with a little oil, place on a baking tray and bake for 5 minutes or until golden brown. Peel the outer skin of the spring garlic and trim the greenest part of the stems. Chop finely and sweat gently in the oil or butter. When nicely softened but not browned, scoop it out of the pan with a slatted spoon and add to the eggs. Season and mix well.

Return the mixture to the pan and cook for a few minutes to make a soft omelette. Cut into triangles small enough to fit on the toasts and serve.

Tortilla con alcachofa y jamón
Artichoke and ham tortilla

Makes 8–10 toasts

1 French stick, cut into 1-cm (½-in) rounds
Olive oil, for brushing
225 g (8 oz) brined artichoke hearts, drained and rinsed
4 slices of jamón, cooked ham, bacon or chorizo
1–2 Tbsp light olive oil
4 eggs, beaten
Salt and freshly ground black pepper
1–2 Tbsp Parmesan or Manchego, grated

Preheat the oven to 190°C (375°F/Gas Mark 5). Brush the bread with a little oil, place on a baking tray and bake for 5 minutes or until golden brown. Roughly chop the artichoke hearts. Cut the jamón, bacon or chorizo into short strips. In a medium pan, gently fry these in the oil for 3 to 4 minutes. Add the artichokes, stir and fry for a further 3 to 4 minutes. Remove with a slatted spoon.

Combine the artichoke mixture with the eggs and season with pepper and a little salt, bearing in mind the saltiness of the jamón or bacon. Sprinkle on the cheese, if using. Return the mixture to the pan and cook for a few minutes to make a soft omelette. Cut into triangles small enough to fit on the toasts and serve.

Tortilla española
Spanish omelette

Makes 24 pinchos

3 large eggs
1 large clove garlic, peeled
750 g (1 lb 11 oz) Maris Piper potatoes, peeled and cubed
500 g (1 lb 2 oz) onions, peeled and diced
500 ml (18 fl oz) oil for frying
Salt

Break the eggs into a bowl and whisk. Finely grate the garlic into the eggs.

Mix the potatoes and onions together in a bowl. Heat the oil in a medium-size non-stick frying pan, add the potato and onion mixture then turn down the heat slightly. Season with salt and stir the mixture regularly, so that it does not stick to the bottom, for 10 minutes or until the potato is cooked. Turn the mixture out into a strainer over a bowl and reserve the oil. After a minute, add the mixture to the eggs and stir thoroughly.

Return the pan to the heat and add just enough of the oil to cover the base in a thin film. Add the egg and potato mixture, spreading it evenly around the pan. Cook over a high heat for about 2 minutes, being careful not to allow it to stick to the bottom. Remove from the heat.

Oil a plate and place it over the frying pan, then carefully invert the pan to reveal a golden brown omelette. Return the pan to the heat, adding a teaspoon of the oil. Slide the tortilla off the plate and into the pan. Cook for a further 1 to 2 minutes. Turn out on to the plate. The golden brown tortilla should be set, yet still soft in the centre and the potatoes crumbly. Cut into eight segments, then cut each segment into three and serve.

Cabrales con nuezes
Blue cheese cream with walnuts

Makes 10–12 toasts

1 French stick, cut into 1-cm (½-in) rounds
2 Tbsp good-quality olive oil
225 g (8 oz) Cabrales, Roquefort, Stilton
or other blue cheese
2 Tbsp single cream, soured cream or crème fraîche
Freshly ground black pepper
50 g (2 oz) walnuts, shelled

Preheat the oven to 190°C (375°F/Gas Mark 5). Brush a little olive oil onto the bread, place on a baking tray and bake for 5 minutes or until golden brown.

In a bowl, crumble the cheese, add the cream and mix together with a fork. It should not be too smooth a mixture. Season with pepper but no salt as the cheese is fairly salty. Spread a teaspoon of the mixture onto the toast and garnish with the walnuts to serve.

Manchego con membrillo
Manchego with quince jelly

Serves 10–12

450 g (1 lb) Manchego or any similar hard or
semi-hard cheese of your choice
450 g (1 lb) membrillo (*see note*)

Cut the cheese into 2-cm (¾-in) cubes. Do the same with
the membrillo or damson cheese if it is stiff enough to
cube. If not, cap each cheese cube with a teaspoonful
of the membrillo. Serve each cube of cheese with the
membrillo on a cocktail stick.

Note: Manchego is the famous hard sheep's cheese from
La Mancha. It is reproduced in other parts of Spain,
often with a mix of sheep's, goat's and cow's milk. It is
often eaten with membrillo, a hard jelly made of quince.
An exquisite, though not strictly Spanish, alternative to
membrillo of similar texture and sweet tartness is damson
cheese, a solid preserve of damsons and sugar.

Pan al ajillo
Garlic French toast

Makes 10–12 toasts

3 large cloves garlic, peeled and minced
1 Tbsp chopped parsley
3 large eggs, beaten
Salt and freshly ground black pepper
1 French stick, cut into 1-cm (½-in) rounds
Olive oil for frying

Add the minced garlic and parsley to the beaten eggs and season well. Allow this to stand for at least half an hour.

Heat the oil in a heavy-bottomed frying pan to about 180°C (350°F). Dip each round of bread in the egg mixture and fry in the pan. Do not fry in batches of more than two or three. Flip over after not much more than 1 minute and cook on the other side for the same amount of time. Drain on kitchen paper and serve at once.

Huevos rellenos
Stuffed eggs

Makes 24

12 small eggs
6 Tbsp mayonnaise
1 tsp mustard
Salt and freshly ground black pepper
6 cherry tomatoes, halved
6 leaves lollo rosso lettuce, torn into 4-cm (1½-in) pieces

Hard-boil the eggs, peel and cut in half lengthways. Scoop out the yolks and mash them together with the mayonnaise and mustard. Season well. Heap the mixture back into the egg halves. Garnish with a halved tomato and a shred of lettuce and serve with cocktail sticks with which to spear the egg halves.

Meat and poultry

Spicy, tasty, quick and easy recipes using beef, chicken, pork, duck and lamb.

Higaditos de pollo con pera
Chicken livers with pears

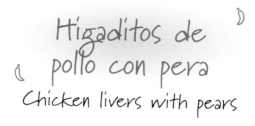

Serves 8–10

50 g (2 oz) flour
2 tsp hot paprika
Salt and freshly ground black pepper
450 g (1 lb) chicken livers, cleaned of membrane
and bile sacs
1 Tbsp light olive oil or 25 g (1 oz) butter
2 cloves garlic, peeled and minced
100 ml (3½ fl oz) brandy
2 ripe pears, peeled, cored and cubed

Put the flour, paprika, generous amounts of salt and pepper into a freezer bag. Add the livers and shake to coat the livers thoroughly.

Heat half the oil or melt half the butter in a medium frying pan and soften the garlic. Turn up the heat and fry half the livers for about 3 to 4 minutes. They should be pink inside. Remove with a slatted spoon and set aside. Add the remaining oil or butter and the other half of the livers and fry. Return the first half of the livers to the pan, increase the heat, then pour on the brandy, set alight and allow to burn out. Serve the livers on cocktail sticks with a piece of pear for every piece of liver.

Tostas de solomillo adobado

Pork fillet toasts

Makes 10–12 toasts

12½ oz (350 g) pork fillet
3 tsp sweet paprika
2 cloves garlic, peeled and minced
1 tsp fresh thyme, chopped
1 tsp sea salt
1 Tbsp good-quality olive oil
1 French baguette, cut into rounds
Olive oil for brushing
6 pimientos de piquillo (see page 23),
halved laterally to make triangles
4 oz (115 g) mozzarella or similar soft cheese,
cut into thin rounds

Cut the tenderloin into 1-cm (1/2-in) thick rounds. Combine the paprika, garlic, thyme, salt and oil in a bowl and add the meat. Mix thoroughly to coat all the meat. Leave to stand for half an hour.

Preheat the oven to 190°C (375°F/Gas Mark 5). Brush a little olive oil onto the bread, then place on a baking tray and bake for 5 minutes or until golden brown.

In a very hot frying or griddle pan, fry the meat for 2 to 3 minutes on either side. Put a piece of the pork on a round of bread, then a piece of pimento, then a slice of cheese. Return the toasts to the oven and bake for just a couple of minutes until the cheese starts to melt. Serve at once.

Albondigas
Veal and pork meatballs

Makes about 24

750 g (1 lb 10 oz) veal mince
250 g (9 oz) pork mince
2 cloves garlic, peeled and crushed
1 small bunch fresh parsley, chopped
150 ml (5 fl oz) milk
5 Tbsp stale breadcrumbs
2 Tbsp light olive oil
3 medium onions, peeled and finely diced
1 Tbsp flour
125 ml (4 fl oz) white wine
Salt and freshly ground black pepper
½ tsp grated nutmeg
2 large eggs, whisked
Flour for dusting
250 ml (8 fl oz) oil for frying

Mix the meats together in a bowl, adding the garlic and parsley and set aside. Pour the milk on to the breadcrumbs. Heat the oil in a pan and soften the onion for 4 to 5 minutes, sprinkle over the flour, stirring continuously, then add the wine and seasoning. Bring to a simmer, then reduce the heat to very low, cooking and stirring for 15 to 20 minutes.

Pass through a sieve and set aside in a casserole. Season the meat with salt, pepper and nutmeg. Squeeze the excess milk from the breadcrumbs and add them to the meat, together with the eggs and three tablespoons of the sauce. Mix thoroughly. Roll the mixture into small balls, then dust with the flour. Heat the oil in a frying pan and fry the meatballs for 5 to 6 minutes, until lightly brown. Remove, drain and transfer to the casserole. Poach the meatballs gently in the sauce for 30 to 40 minutes, until they are tender and the sauce is very thick. Serve warm.

Riñones al jérez
Kidneys in sherry

Serves 8–10

450 g (1 lb) lamb's kidneys
3 Tbsp light olive oil
3 cloves garlic, peeled and finely chopped
115 g (4 oz) mushrooms, chopped
2–3 slices of jamón or bacon, cut into strips
Salt and freshly ground black pepper
225 ml (8 fl oz) dry sherry
1 Tbsp parsley, chopped

Use a very sharp knife to remove the membrane from the kidneys. Cut them in half lengthways and remove and discard the cores by snipping them out with scissors. Cut them in half again and, if you wish, stand them in cold, salted water.

Heat 2 tablespoonsful of the oil in a heavy frying pan and soften the garlic for a couple of minutes. Add the mushrooms and jamón and fry for 8 to 10 minutes until the mixture is fairly dry. Remove with a slatted spoon and set aside.Add the rest of the oil and fry the kidneys for 2 to 3 minutes. Be careful not to overcook them, they should be pinkish inside. Return the mushrooms and jamón to the pan, season and add the sherry. Increase the heat and bring to the boil, cooking until most of the liquid has evaporated. Sprinkle with the parsley and serve as trios of kidney, mushroom and jamón on cocktail sticks.

Note: Lamb's kidneys may be unfamiliar territory for many, but you should not be daunted. Once cleaned, they can be stood in cold, slightly salted water for a couple of hours to achieve a milder taste.

Albondigas de pollo
Chicken meatballs

Makes 24

900 g (2 lb) chicken breasts, diced
150 g (5 oz) streaky bacon, diced
3 cloves garlic, peeled and crushed
1 bunch fresh parsley, chopped
100 g (3½ oz) olives, diced
150 ml (5 fl oz) milk
5 Tbsp stale breadcrumbs
2 onions, peeled and diced
2 tsp light olive oil
1 large egg, beaten
Salt and freshly ground black pepper
Flour for dusting
250 ml (8 fl oz) oil for frying
400 g (14 oz) tinned chopped tomatoes
125 ml (4 fl oz) white wine
1 bay leaf
250 ml (8 fl oz) chicken stock

Put the chicken, bacon, half the garlic, half the parsley and olives in a food processor and whizz briefly. Pour the milk on to the breadcrumbs, squeeze out the excess milk and add them to the meat, along with one of the onions, softened in the olive oil and the egg. Season with salt and pepper then mix and form into balls, dust with flour.

Heat the oil in a frying pan and fry the balls for 5 to 6 minutes, until lightly brown. Remove, drain and transfer to the casserole. Pour off all but 1 tablespoon of the oil and use this to soften the remaining onion for 4 to 5 minutes. Add the tomatoes, remaining garlic and parsley, wine and bay leaf. Simmer for 10 minutes before adding the stock. Add the meatballs to the sauce and simmer gently for 30 minutes. Serve warm.

Patatas con chorizo
Potatoes with chorizo

Serves 8–10

1 kg (2 lb 3 oz) salad or new potatoes
1 Tbsp light olive oil
225 g (8 oz) chorizo, cut into 1-cm (½-in) thick rounds
1 medium onion, peeled and
cut into 2-cm (¾-in) triangles
2 red or green peppers, cored and
cut into 2-cm (¾-in) triangles
2 Tbsp passata (creamed and sieved tomatoes)
Salt and freshly ground black pepper

Scrub the potatoes clean, place them in a large saucepan of cold, salted water and bring gently to the boil. Simmer for 15 minutes or until they are cooked through. Remove from the heat, drain and set aside.

Heat the oil in a large frying pan, add the chorizo and fry until it releases its melting pimentón-red fat. After a couple of minutes, add the onion to soften, then the peppers. Cut the potatoes into 2-cm (¾-in) thick rounds. Add to the pan, increase the heat and cook through for a few minutes, stirring carefully so as not to break them up. Add the sieved tomatoes, lower the heat, season and simmer until the sauce thickens. Serve the potatoes, chorizo, peppers and onions threaded onto sticks.

Pinchos morunos
Pork brochettes

Makes about 20

900 g (2 lb) loin of pork, cut into 2-cm (¾-in) cubes
50 ml (2 fl oz) white wine
50 ml (2 fl oz) light olive oil
3 large cloves garlic, peeled and crushed
2 tsp hot smoked paprika, chilli powder or cayenne
pepper (or 1 tsp of hot smoked paprika,
chilli powder or cayenne pepper and 1 tsp
mild smoked paprika, if you prefer)
½ bay leaf, crumbled
2 tsp chopped fresh thyme
Salt and freshly ground black pepper
2 lemons, quartered (optional)

Arrange the meat in a wide, shallow, non-metallic dish.
Mix together all the other ingredients, except the lemons,
and season. Pour the mixture over the meat, cover and
leave to marinate, preferably in the fridge, for at least
8 hours, turning once or twice.

Thread three cubes onto a skewer and cook on a very hot
griddle or grill, turning once or twice, for about 8 minutes.
The meat will be charred slightly, but still juicy. Squeeze over
the juice of the lemon wedges, if you wish, and serve hot.

Delicias de pato al calvados

Calvados duck breasts

Makes 12 tartlets

250 g (9oz) ready-made puff pastry
Flour for dusting
1 Tbsp light olive oil or 25 g (1 oz) butter
2 duck breasts, skinned and diced
2 cloves garlic, peeled and minced
1 large or 2 small tart apples, peeled, cored, diced and
tossed in a little lemon juice to prevent discoloration
100 ml (3½ fl oz) calvados or other brandy

Preheat the oven to 190°C (375°F/Gas Mark 5). Roll out
the pastry onto a floured board and use to line 12 tartlet
moulds. Place in the oven and cook for about 5 minutes or
until the pastry turns golden and starts to puff up. Remove
from the oven and keep warm.

Heat the oil or butter in a medium frying pan and fry the
duck pieces for a couple of minutes. Remove with a slatted
spoon and keep warm. Add the garlic to soften in the pan
before adding the diced apple. Stir briefly and add the
duck. Increase the heat then add the calvados. Set alight
and allow to burn out. Heap spoonsful of the mixture on
the still warm pastry tartlets and serve immediately.

Tartaletas hongos y jamón
Ham and mushroom tartlets

Makes 12 tartlets

250 g (9 oz) ready-made puff pastry
Flour for dusting
1 Tbsp light olive oil
1 Tbsp shallots, finely diced
1 large clove garlic, peeled and crushed
250 g (9 oz) mixed wild mushrooms, chopped
100 g (3½ oz) jamón, diced
100 ml (3½ fl oz) dry white wine
1 Tbsp finely chopped fresh parsley

Preheat the oven to 190°C (370°F/Gas Mark 5). Roll the pastry out onto a floured board and use to line 12 tartlet moulds. Place in the oven and cook for about 5 minutes or until the pastry turns golden and starts to puff up. Remove from the oven and allow to cool.

Heat the oil in a frying pan and soften the shallots and garlic for 2 to 3 minutes. Add the mushrooms and jamón. After a minute or two, add the wine and bring up to a simmer for 7 to 8 minutes. Spoon the mixture into the tartlets, sprinkle over the parsley and serve.

Carne guisada con patatitas
Beef with fried potatoes

Serves 10–12

1 kg (2 lb 3 oz) stewing steak, cubed
Salt and freshly ground black pepper
4 cloves garlic, peeled and minced
1 kg (2 lb 3 oz) salad or new potatoes,
cut into 2-cm (½-in) rounds
3 Tbsp light olive oil
1 large Spanish onion, finely chopped
1 large red pepper, diced
1 Tbsp parsley, chopped
1 slice of dry toast
50 ml (2 fl oz) dry white wine
50 ml (2 fl oz) water
Oil for frying

Season the meat with salt and pepper and add 3 of the cloves of garlic. Mix well and leave to macerate for 1 hour in the fridge. Season the raw potatoes and set aside.

Heat the oil to high in a casserole and brown the meat in batches, returning it all to the pan at the end. Turn down the heat and add the onion and pepper. Stir and add the remaining garlic, the parsley and crumble in the toast, so that you achieve a fairly thick sauce. Add the wine and water, cover and simmer gently until tender, for up to half an hour.

Heat the frying oil to 160°C (325°F) and fry the potatoes until golden brown, turning carefully every so often. When they are done, remove with a slatted spoon and add to the meat, mixing carefully but not cooking any further. Serve pieces of meat and potato on cocktail sticks.

Croquetas de jamón
Ham croquettes

Makes about 36

100 g (3½ oz) butter
125 g (4 oz) plain flour
600 ml (1 pint) cold milk
200 g (7 oz) jamón, cut into strips
Salt and freshly ground black pepper
5 or 6 Tbsp fine breadcrumbs
2 large eggs, beaten
Oil for deep-frying

Melt the butter in a medium saucepan and add the flour, stirring continuously. Allow the flour to cook in the butter for a couple of minutes, stirring continuously. Add the cold milk little by little, stirring all the while until you have a thick, smooth sauce. Add the jamón and season well. Continue to cook for 7 or 8 minutes, then allow the mixture to cool completely.

Take a scant tablespoon of the mixture and form into a croquette, a 3–4 cm (1½–2 in) cylinder. Roll the croquette in the breadcrumbs, then coat in the beaten egg and roll in the breadcrumbs again. Make sure the breadcrumbs are always dry to ensure an even coating.

Heat the oil in a large, heavy-based pan until the temperature reaches 180°C (350°F). Fry in batches of no more than 3 or 4 for about 5 minutes until golden brown. Remove with a slatted spoon, drain on kitchen paper and serve immediately.

Cochifrito
Lamb with lemon sauce

Serves 8–10

900 g (2 lb) lean lamb,
cut into 5 x 2.5-cm (2 x 1-in) pieces
Salt and freshly ground black pepper
Juice of 2 lemons
2 Tbsp light olive oil
1 onion, peeled and finely chopped
2 cloves garlic, peeled and minced
2 tsp paprika
2 Tbsp parsley, finely chopped
100 ml (3½ fl oz) water

Place the meat in a bowl, season and pour over the lemon juice. Place it in the fridge to macerate for 1 hour.

Heat the oil in a casserole to high and fry small batches of the meat, squeezed of the marinade, until it browns. Remove with a slatted spoon and set aside.

Add the onion to the pan, then the garlic and soften for 3 to 4 minutes. Return the meat to the pan, sprinkle with paprika and parsley, then add the remains of the marinade and the water. Bring back to a simmer and cook for a further 7 to 8 minutes, by which time the juices will have reduced down to a thick coating on the meat. Thread two or three well-coated strips onto each cocktail stick.

Pinchos de lomo con castañas

Pork tenderloin with chestnuts

Serves 6–8

500 g (1 lb 2 oz) pork tenderloin,
cut into 2-cm (¾-in) pieces
Salt and freshly ground black pepper
2 cloves garlic, peeled and minced
50 ml (2 fl oz) dry sherry
1 Tbsp light olive oil
200 g (7 oz) chestnuts
50 ml (2 fl oz) brandy
2 tsp hot paprika

Season the meat with salt and pepper, add the garlic and sherry, mix well and allow to marinate for at least half an hour.

Heat the oil in a large frying pan, turn up the heat and brown the meat in two batches, for 4 to 5 minutes. Return all the meat to the pan, add the chestnuts and leftover marinade juices. Pour on the brandy and set alight. When the alcohol burns out, sprinkle on the paprika. Poach for a few more minutes until the juices have all evaporated. Serve a chunk of pork with a chestnut on a cocktail stick.

Pincho de cordero
Lamb brochettes

Makes about 20

900 g (2 lb) lamb neck fillet, cut into 2-cm (¾-in) cubes
50 ml (2 fl oz) white wine
50 ml (2 fl oz) light olive oil
½ tsp chilli powder or cayenne pepper
½ tsp ground cumin
½ tsp turmeric
½ tsp ground coriander
½ tsp ground ginger
3 cloves garlic, peeled and crushed
Salt and freshly ground black pepper
2 lemons, quartered (optional)

Arrange the meat in a wide, shallow, non-metallic dish.
Mix together all the other ingredients, except the lemons,
and season. Pour the mixture over the meat, cover and
leave to marinate, preferably in the fridge, for at least
8 hours, turning once or twice.

Thread the meat onto skewers and cook on a very hot
griddle or grill, turning once or twice, for about 8 minutes.
Serve hot, with the quartered lemons.

Pollo al ajillo
Garlic chicken

Serves 8–10

1.5-kg (3 lb 5-oz) whole chicken
6–8 cloves garlic, peeled and minced
2 Tbsp parsley, finely chopped
Salt and freshly ground black pepper
3 Tbsp plain flour
Oil for deep frying

Cut the chicken into about twenty 4-cm (1½-in) pieces, including the backbone and the parson's nose. This is for people who love fried chicken on the bone! Put the chicken pieces into a ceramic bowl, add the garlic and parsley and season generously. Mix together thoroughly – the best way is to work seasoning into the chicken with your hands, not so bad once you take the plunge. The seasoning must be given time to work on the meat, so allow it to stand in the fridge for several hours, or even overnight.

Put the flour into a plastic freezer bag and add 5 or 6 pieces of chicken. Shake well so that the chicken is thickly coated with the flour. In a large saucepan, heat the oil to 200°C (400°F) and drop in the first batch of chicken pieces and fry until golden brown, for about 8 to 10 minutes. Remove with a slatted spoon and drain on kitchen paper. Serve immediately.

Pincho de pollo
Chicken brochettes

Makes about 20

900 g (2 lb) chicken or turkey breast, cut into
2-cm (¾-in) cubes
50 ml (2 fl oz) light olive oil
3 cloves garlic, peeled and crushed
1 small bunch fresh parsley, chopped
Salt and freshly ground black pepper
2 lemons

Mix together the olive oil, garlic, chopped parsley, salt and pepper and the juice of half a lemon to make a persillade. Marinate the meat in the persillade for 1 to 2 hours.

Thread the chicken pieces onto skewers and cook on a very hot griddle or grill, turning once or twice, for about 6 minutes. Serve hot, with the quartered lemons.

Pollo a la cazadora
Huntsman's chicken

Serves 10–12

1.5 kg (3 lb 5 oz) whole chicken, cut into 20 pieces,
including backbone
Salt and freshly ground black pepper
3 cloves garlic, peeled and minced
3 Tbsp light olive oil
Liver from the chicken (optional)
1 medium onion, peeled and finely chopped
1 bay leaf
1 bunch parsley stalks, chopped
115 ml (4 fl oz) brandy
1 Tbsp toasted almonds, ground
2 Tbsp light olive oil
20 button mushrooms

Season the chicken and add the garlic, mixing thoroughly and allowing to macerate for 1 hour in the fridge.

Heat the oil in a casserole to high, add the chicken in batches and cook until well browned. Turn down the heat and return all the chicken pieces to the casserole. Add the liver, if using, onion, bay leaf, parsley stalks, brandy and sprinkle with the almonds. Stir well, cover and stew gently for 12 to 15 minutes.

Remove the chicken pieces with a slatted spoon and set aside. Take out the liver and chop finely before returning to the casserole. To make a sauce, purée the contents of the pan (including the liver, if using). A hand-held blender is best for this.

Heat the remaining oil in a frying pan and sauté the mushrooms for 2 to 3 minutes. Return the chicken to the casserole along with the sauce and add the mushrooms. Continue to heat until the sauce has thickened enough to coat the chicken and mushrooms. Serve a piece of chicken with a mushroom on a cocktail stick.

Chorizo al vino
Chorizo in red wine

Serves 10

10 chorizo sausages
400 ml (14 fl oz) robust red wine

Preheat the oven to 200°C (400°F/Gas Mark 6). Put
the chorizo sausages into a roasting pan and pour the
wine over. Roast in the oven for about 40 minutes.
The sausages should be browned and slightly crispy,
the wine all but evaporated. Cut each chorizo into
3 or 4 pieces and serve hot.

Champiñon, gamba, iberico
Mushroom, prawn and ham sticks

Makes 12

12 button mushrooms, stalks removed
50 ml (2 fl oz) light olive oil
Juice of ½ lemon
1 large clove garlic, peeled and crushed
75 ml (3 fl oz) dry white wine
12 cooked prawns, peeled
50 g (2 oz) jamón, cut into strips
1 Tbsp finely chopped fresh parsley

Simmer the mushrooms gently in a little salted water, adding 2 teaspoons of the oil and the lemon juice, for 7 to 8 minutes. Drain and allow to cool.

Heat the remaining oil and fry the garlic until golden. Arrange the mushrooms on a serving dish and sprinkle with the wine. Thread a prawn and a strip of jamón onto a cocktail stick before spearing the mushroom. Pour over the garlic-flavoured oil and sprinkle with the parsley.

Note: Spanish cooks add refrito – finely diced garlic fried in olive oil – as a finish to many simple dishes, often soups and pulses. It gives an aromatic flavour boost to otherwise bland fare.

Solomillo con salsa de berros

Fillet steak with watercress cream sauce

Serves 8–10

1 Tbsp good-quality olive oil
2 shallots, peeled and chopped finely
150 ml (5 fl oz) dry white wine
1 bunch watercress
150 ml (5 fl oz) double cream or crème fraîche
1 Tbsp mild mustard
Salt and freshly ground black pepper
700 g (1 lb 9 oz) fillet steak
Olive oil for brushing

Heat the oil in a frying pan and soften the shallots for a couple of minutes. Add the wine and the watercress, and poach for five minutes, allowing the alcohol to evaporate. Pour in the cream, stir in the mustard and season. Simmer gently for a further 5 to 6 minutes. Purée (easiest with a handheld blender) and correct the seasoning, if necessary.

Heat a griddle pan to very hot, brush the steaks with oil, season with pepper and cook them to your taste. Season with salt and allow to stand for several minutes. Pour the sauce over the steaks, cut them into quarters and serve on cocktail sticks

Fish and seafood

Croquettes, brochettes and tartlets, all made using the freshest fish and seafood.

Txitxarro
Mackerel and leek toasts

Makes 12

1 French stick, cut into 1-cm (½-in) rounds
Olive oil for brushing
1 medium mackerel, cleaned and gutted
2 Tbsp of light olive oil
1 medium leek, finely sliced
1 medium onion, peeled and finely sliced
1 bay leaf
100 ml (3½ fl oz) dry white wine
1 Tbsp sherry vinegar
Salt and freshly ground black pepper

Preheat the oven to 190°C (375°F/Gas Mark 5). Brush a little olive oil onto the bread, place on a baking tray and bake for 5 minutes or until golden brown. Remove from the oven and set aside.

Increase the heat to 230°C (450°F/Gas Mark 8) and roast the mackerel for 8 to 10 minutes. Skin and then bone the cooled mackerel and set aside.

In a frying pan, soften the leek and onion in the oil with the bay leaf. Add the wine and vinegar and poach for 8 to 10 minutes, allowing the liquid to evaporate. Remove and discard the bay leaf and season. Layer the toasted bread with the sautéed leek, follow with the mackerel and finally more leek.

Langostino guacamole
Prawn and guacamole toasts

Makes 12

1 French stick, cut into 1-cm (½-in) rounds
Olive oil for brushing
1 large, ripe avocado, roughly mashed
1 large tomato, peeled, deseeded and diced
1 spring onion, finely diced
1 tsp chopped fresh coriander
Salt and freshly ground black pepper
3 medium potatoes, boiled and sliced in four
125 ml (4 fl oz) garlic mayonnaise
12 large prawns, cooked

Preheat the oven to 190°C (375°F/Gas Mark 5). Brush a little olive oil onto the bread, place on a baking tray and bake for 5 minutes or until golden brown.

To make the guacamole, mix the avocado, tomato, spring onion and coriander together. Season well. In a separate bowl, coat the potatoes with the mayonnaise and place on the bread. Heap some guacamole on top and garnish with a prawn.

Croquetas de pescado
Fish croquettes

Makes 20

450 g (1 lb) floury potatoes, e.g. King Edward
500 g (1 lb 2 oz) fish of your choice,
e.g. cod, haddock, hake or salmon
300 ml (11 fl oz) milk or fish stock
1 Tbsp light olive oil
1 large onion, peeled and finely diced
2 cloves garlic, peeled and crushed
1 tsp hot smoked paprika
3 large eggs
1 bunch fresh parsley, finely chopped
Salt and freshly ground black pepper
1–2 Tbsp flour
2–3 Tbsp fine breadcrumbs
350 ml (12 fl oz) oil for frying

Boil the potatoes then drain, mash and set aside. Gently poach the fish in milk or fish stock (the latter is best for salmon), bringing to a simmer for about 3 to 4 minutes. Allow the fish to cool, then remove any skin and bones and flake with a fork.

Soften the onion in the olive oil for 3 to 4 minutes before adding the garlic and paprika. Beat one of the eggs in a bowl and add the flaked fish to it, along with the softened onion and parsley. Season generously and then carefully fold the mixture into the potatoes.

Making sure the fish keeps its shape, take small tablespoonfuls of the mixture and form into balls. Coat in flour. Whisk the remaining eggs, with a little milk if you like. Roll the balls first in the egg and then the breadcrumbs. Shallow-fry the croquettes in hot oil until crisp and golden. Serve with aïoli (see page 42), if liked.

Ceviche de salmon
Marinated salmon

Serves 10

450 g (1 lb) salmon fillet, skinned
(monkfish, halibut or turbot are also excellent)
1 medium red onion, peeled and very thinly sliced
Juice of 2 lemons
1 Tbsp light olive oil
½ tsp hot smoked paprika, chilli powder
or cayenne pepper
1 hot red chilli, finely chopped
Salt and freshly ground black pepper
2–3 Tbsp chopped fresh parsley, coriander or chives
20 cherry tomatoes, halved
1 small pepper, deseeded and cut into 2-cm (1-in) triangles

Wrap the salmon in foil or clingfilm and put in the freezer
for up to 1 hour. This makes slicing the fish much easier.
Slice the fish very thinly, using a sharp knife.

In a shallow, wide non-metallic dish, place the onion,
lemon juice, oil, paprika and chilli. Season generously then
add the fish, turning to coat all over. Leave to marinate in
the fridge if you wish, for a couple of hours, depending
how 'rare' you want the fish. This will also depend on how
thinly you have sliced it. Add your choice of herb minutes
before you assemble the pincho. Sandwich one or two
slices of the fish between a tomato half and a pepper
triangle and serve immediately.

Calamares rebozados
Battered squid

Serves 8–10

450 g (1 lb) squid
1 large egg, beaten
150 g (5½ oz) flour
Salt and freshly ground black pepper
Oil for frying
2 lemons, quartered

Cut off the tentacles and reserve. Clean the squid by reaching into the sac and pulling out as much as possible. Discard what you have pulled out. Pull off the two outside flaps and set aside. Rub the sac with salted hands to clean the outside of the purplish skin and to loosen what remains inside. Thoroughly rinse the sac under cold running water, inside and out. Pull out the clear, flexible spine. Cut the sac into 1.5-cm (½-in) rings. Rinse the rings, flaps and tentacles again.

Sift the flour into the beaten egg gradually, whisking as you go. Season with salt and pepper, then whisk again. You should achieve a batter the consistency of jam. Fold in the squid gently.

Heat enough oil to 180°C (350°F/Gas Mark 4) and fry the squid in small batches until golden. Serve with the quartered lemons.

Sardinas fritas
Fried sardines

Makes 10

350 ml (12 fl oz) oil for frying
2 Tbsp flour
Salt and freshly ground black pepper
10 sardines, not longer than 15–20 cm (6–8 in)
1 large lemon, quartered

Heat the oil in a heavy-based frying pan, large enough to take 2 or 3 sardines. Put the flour in a plastic bag and season with the salt and pepper. Drop the sardines into the bag and shake well to coat. Lift out, shaking off the excess flour. Fry the sardines in the hot oil for 1 to 2 minutes on each side. Squeeze over the juice from the lemon wedges.

Note: To give the fish a characteristically Spanish tang, add 2 teaspoons of hot smoked paprika or chilli powder to the flour. For a Moorish flavour, add 1 teaspoon each of ground turmeric and ground cumin to the flour.

Montado casa vergara
Seafood toasts

Makes 12

1 French stick, cut into 1-cm (½-in) rounds
2 Tbsp good-quality olive oil
2 Tbsp mayonnaise
200 g (7 oz) smoked salmon or trout
12 marinated anchovies (boquerones, see page 21)
3 Tbsp vinagreta (see page 158)
24 small prawns

Preheat the oven to 190°C (375°F/Gas Mark 5). Brush a little olive oil onto the bread, place on a baking tray and bake for 5 minutes or until golden brown.

Spread the toasted bread slices with a little of the mayonnaise. Layer the smoked fish and marinated anchovies, dress with the vinagreta, arrange a couple of the prawns and top it all off with a little mayonnaise.

Pimientos rellenos de bacalao

Salt cod-stuffed pimentos

Makes 12

1 French stick
Olive oil for brushing
100 g (3½ oz) butter
125 g (4½ oz) flour
600 ml (1 pint) cold milk
Salt and freshly ground black pepper
2 Tbsp olive oil
1 medium onion, finely chopped
1 green pepper, finely chopped
450 g (1 lb) bacalao (salt cod), desalinated, deboned, skinned and flaked
1 Tbsp parsley, finely chopped
12 pimientos de piquillo (see page 21)

Preheat the oven to 190°C (375°F/Gas Mark 5). Slice the French stick into 1-cm (½-in) rounds and brush with a little oil. Place on a baking tray and bake in the oven for about 5 minutes, or until golden brown.

In the meantime, make a béchamel sauce. Melt the butter in a medium saucepan and add the flour, stirring continuously. Allow the flour to cook in the butter for a couple of minutes, stirring continuously. Add the cold milk little by little, stirring all the while until you have a thick, smooth sauce. Season and allow to cool.

In a medium frying pan, soften the onion and pepper in the olive oil for 3 to 4 minutes. Add the bacalao and cook for a further 3 minutes, stirring gently, then add the parsley. Scoop out the fish mixture with a slatted spoon and fold into the béchamel.

Drain the pimentos and fill them with the salt cod mixture. Thread a cocktail stick through the mouth of the pimentos to prevent leakage. Return the pimentos to the oil in the pan and warm through. Serve on the toasted French bread.

Note: Bacalao is cod which has been preserved by being salted and dried. The success of salt cod depends very much on the quality of the fish more than anything else. Try to avoid buying thin, meagre pieces: the plumper, the better. Before using it, it needs thorough desalination – you must use plenty of water and allow at least 24 hours to complete the process. Soak in clean, fresh water and change the water about three or four times, then drain and pat the piece dry. You should be able to skin the fish quite easily and there will be bones to pick out (use tweezers to remove the tiniest of these).

Brochetas de gambas y bacon

Prawn and bacon brochettes

Makes 12

150 g (5½ oz) jamón or thinly sliced bacon
24 medium to large uncooked, headless prawns, peeled
Freshly ground black pepper
1 Tbsp light olive oil
2 lemons, quartered

Cut the jamón into pieces which will wrap generously around the prawns. Place the wrapped prawns on a board and skewer them through the fattest part and the tail, making sure the jamón is firmly fixed. Season generously and drizzle with the oil.

On a high heat, griddle, grill or barbecue the brochettes for 2 to 3 minutes on each side, so the jamón crisps up. Alternatively, roast in a hot oven (220˚C/425˚F/Gas Mark 7) on an oiled baking tray for 8 to 10 minutes. Squeeze over the juice of the lemon wedges and serve immediately.

Tartaleta de salmon, esparragos y alcachofa
Salmon, asparagus and artichoke tartlet

Makes 12 tartlets

250 g (9 oz) ready-made puff pastry
Flour for dusting
250 g (9 oz) salmon fillet, thinly sliced
1 Tbsp sugar
1 Tbsp salt
1 Tbsp finely chopped fresh herbs, such as parsley,
dill or chervil
200 g (7 oz) fine asparagus tips
100 g (3½ oz) tinned artichoke hearts
100 ml (3½ fl oz) oil for frying

Preheat the oven to 190°C (375°F/Gas Mark 5). Roll the pastry out onto a floured board and use to line 12 tartlet moulds. Place in the oven and cook for about 5 minutes or until the pastry turns golden and starts to puff up. Remove from the oven and allow to cool.

Place the salmon in the freezer for ½ hour to make it easier to slice thinly. Lay the slices out on a dish, sprinkle with sugar, salt and the herbs, cover and leave to marinate for 2 hours, turning once or twice.

Brush the salmon clean with a pastry brush and set aside. Drop the asparagus into boiling salted water, bring back to the boil and simmer for 1 to 2 minutes. Refresh in iced water, drain and set aside. Slice the artichokes finely and fry them in the oil until crisp.

Heat a heavy-based frying pan and sear the salmon for 30 seconds on each side. Place a slice of the salmon, followed by 2 to 3 asparagus tips, then an artichoke slice into the tartlet and serve.

Gilda frutos del mar
Seafood sticks

Makes 12

285-g (10-oz) jar seafood in oil and vinegar
285-g (10-oz) jar guindilla chillies (see page 21)
115 g (4 oz) tinned mussels in escabeche (see page 24)

Assemble a morsel or two of the seafood, followed by two
or three small guindilla chillies and finally a plump mussel.

Note: Seafood in oil and vinegar, often labelled 'antipasto',
is available in supermarkets.

Boquerones en vinagreta
Marinated anchovy sticks

Makes 12

36 marinated anchovies (boquerones)
12 pimento-, almond- or lemon-stuffed olives
1 large clove garlic, peeled and crushed
1 Tbsp extra-virgin olive oil
2 tsp finely chopped fresh parsley

Thread three folded marinated anchovies onto a cocktail stick, followed by an olive. Mix together the garlic, olive oil and parsley and drizzle over the anchovies.

Tartaleta de bacalao
Salt cod tartlet

Makes 12 tartlets

250 g (9 oz) ready-made puff pastry
Flour for dusting
175 ml (6 fl oz) light olive oil for frying
2 cloves garlic, peeled and crushed
2 red peppers, cut into broad strips
2 green peppers, cut into broad strips
450 g (1 lb) bacalao or smoked haddock, skin on
Salt and freshly ground black pepper
1 lemon, quartered

Preheat the oven to 190°C (370°F/Gas Mark 5). Roll the pastry out onto a floured board and use to line 12 tartlet moulds. Place in the oven and cook for about 5 minutes or until the pastry turns golden and starts to puff up. Remove from the oven and allow to cool.

Heat 2 tablespoons of the oil in a frying pan and add the crushed garlic and the pepper strips. Gently cook the pepper strips until soft, for about 10 to 12 minutes. Remove, allow to cool then peel off the skin.

Add the remaining oil to the pan. Place the fish, skin side down, gently in the oil and fry for about 6 or 7 minutes, shaking the pan every few seconds towards the end to release the gelatin from under the skin. Lift the fish out of the pan, remove the skin and bones and flake it. Fill the tartlets with fish, garnish with the pepper strips, season and daub with a little of the gelatin-thickened sauce. Sprinkle over a little juice from the lemon wedges, if you wish, and serve.

Ceviche tres mares

Three-seas ceviche

Serves 10

1 large onion, peeled and thinly sliced
450 g (1 lb) monkfish, sliced into 5-cm (2-in) pieces
1 red chilli, seeded and diced
Water from 1 fresh coconut
Juice of 4 limes
100 ml (3½ fl oz) extra-virgin olive oil
1 bunch fresh parsley, chopped
1 avocado, cut into cubes
20 cherry tomatoes

Place a layer of onion and then a layer of fish in a large shallow dish. Sprinkle with a little diced chilli. Repeat these layers, finishing with a layer of onion.

Drain the water from the coconut and strain it. Add to the fish and onion along with the lime juice, making sure the liquid reaches the top. Stir gently, cover and marinate for at least 6 hours or overnight if the fish is thickly sliced. Lift the fish from the marinade and pat dry on kitchen paper. Transfer to a dish, add the olive oil and herbs and stir thoroughly, leaving it to stand for at least 1 hour. Assemble the pincho by threading the avocado, fish and tomato onto cocktail sticks.

Mejillones marinera
Mussels in white wine sauce

Serves 8–10

900 g (2 lb) mussels
1 Tbsp olive oil
1 medium onion, peeled and chopped
2 cloves garlic, peeled and chopped
250 ml (9 fl oz) dry white wine
1 Tbsp parsley, chopped
Salt and freshly ground black pepper

Clean the mussels by scrubbing, 'de-bearding' and rinsing in plenty of cold running water. Discard any cracked shells and those mussels which remain open when you tap them.

In a saucepan, soften the onion and garlic for a minute or two in the olive oil before adding the wine and half the parsley. Allow the alcohol to evaporate by simmering for 10 minutes. Add the mussels, cover with a lid and continue to simmer for a further 5 minutes. It is important to shake the saucepan every minute to allow all the mussels to cook through evenly.

Drain the mussels, reserving the liquid. This can be reduced to taste by simmering. Allow the mussels to cool just enough to handle, then break off and discard the empty half-shells. Any unopened mussels must also be discarded. Pour over the reheated liquid, season and serve.

Croquetas de gambas
Prawn croquettes

Makes about 36

100 g (3½ oz) butter
125 g (4½ oz) plain flour
600 ml (1 pint) cold milk
400 g (14 oz) cooked peeled prawns, diced
Salt and freshly ground black pepper
2 tsp tomato purée
5 or 6 Tbsp fine breadcrumbs
2 large eggs, beaten
Oil for deep-frying

Melt the butter in a medium saucepan and add the flour, stirring continuously. Allow the flour to cook in the butter for a couple of minutes, stirring continuously. Add the cold milk little by little, stirring all the while until you have a thick, smooth sauce. Add the prawns, season well and stir in the tomato purée. Continue to cook for 7 or 8 minutes. The end result should be quite thick. It is essential that the mixture is allowed to cool completely.

Take a scant tablespoon of the mixture and form into a croquette, a 3–4 cm (1½–2 in) cylinder. Roll the croquette in the breadcrumbs, then coat in the beaten egg and roll in the breadcrumbs again. Make sure the breadcrumbs are always dry to ensure an even coating.

Heat the oil in a large, heavy-based pan until the temperature reaches 180°C (350°F). Fry in batches of no more than 3 or 4 for about 5 minutes until golden brown. Remove with a slatted spoon, drain on kitchen paper and serve immediately.

Ceviche de vieiras
Scallop ceviche

Serves 8

8 large scallops
2 shallots, peeled and very finely diced
1 small chilli, finely chopped
Juice of 4 limes
Juice of 2 oranges
Salt
1 Tbsp parsley or coriander, finely chopped

Slice the scallops in half horizontally. In a bowl, add the shallots and chilli to the lime and orange juices. Add the scallops, including their orange roe crescents, and season with the salt. Mix together thoroughly and place in the fridge to marinate for 4 to 5 hour.

Serve on cocktail sticks, sprinkled with parsley or coriander, with a little of the marinade scooped over them.

Note: Raw, fresh scallops, now usually sold cleaned, are marinated, here in lime and orange juice. For an authentic Spanish Caribbean variation, you can substitute coconut water for the orange juice. Shake it and listen for the splash of the water inside. If you hear nothing, it will be dry!

Tartaletas de bonito y gamba
Tuna tartlets

Makes 12 tartlets

250 g (9 oz) ready-made puff pastry
Flour for dusting
2 Tbsp light olive oil
25 ml (1 fl oz) white wine vinegar
Salt and freshly ground black pepper
1 Tbsp spring onion or shallot, very finely chopped
4 ripe medium tomatoes
225 g (8 oz) bonito or other best quality tuna,
preserved in olive oil (drained weight)
12 prawns, cooked and peeled.

Preheat the oven to 190°C(375°F/Gas Mark 5). Roll out
the pastry on a floured board and use it to line 12 tartlet
moulds. Place in the oven and cook for about 5 minutes
or until the pastry turns golden and starts to puff up.
Remove from the oven and keep warm.

Make a vinaigrette by whisking the oil (be sure to add the
oil drained from the jar of bonito as well as the olive oil)
and vinegar, season and stir in the spring onion or shallot.
Slice the tomatoes into 12 rounds and place one in each of
the tartlets. Divide the tuna among the tartlets, so that
there is a generous heap in each. Garnish with a prawn and
spoon some of the vinaigrette on top.

Rape en salsa de almendras
Monkfish with almond sauce

Serves 8–10

4 Tbsp light olive oil
1 medium onion, peeled and finely chopped
2 cloves garlic, peeled and minced
Scant 1 kg (2 lb) monkfish tail fillet
Salt and freshly ground black pepper
75 g (2½ oz) blanched almonds, ground
2 Tbsp water
2 Tbsp dry white wine
1 Tbsp parsley, finely chopped
Juice of ½ lemon

Heat half the oil in a casserole, add the onion, then the garlic and soften for 3 to 4 minutes. Cut the fish into 2-cm (¾-in) cubes, add to the onion and season. Pour in the remaining oil and gently fry the fish for 2 to 3 minutes, turning carefully once or twice. Remove the fish from the casserole with a slatted spoon and set aside.

In a bowl, mix together the almonds, water, wine and parsley, and pour into the casserole with the onions. Cook for 2 to 3 minutes, until the sauce starts to thicken. Return the fish to the casserole and cook for a further 3 to 4 minutes before adding the lemon juice. The fish should be well coated with the almond sauce. Serve on cocktail sticks, spooning over the remains of the sauce.

Gildas
Anchovy, olive and guindilla sticks

Makes about 12

100 g (3½ oz) marinated anchovies in olive oil
285 g (10 oz) guindilla chillies (see page 21),
cut into 2-cm (¾-in) pieces
225 g (8 oz) pitted green olives

Curl up each anchovy and thread it onto a cocktail stick, along with two or three guindilla chillies and an olive. Stack the gilda onto a plate and serve immediately.

Ostras vinagreta
Oysters with shallot vinaigrette

Makes 12

12 oysters
100 ml (3½ fl oz) olive oil
25 ml (1 fl oz) red wine vinegar
Salt and freshly ground black pepper
4 shallots, peeled and finely chopped

To open the oysters, a proper shucking knife is best.
A short, dagger-pointed, robust knife can substitute.
To open, place the oyster on a board, flat side up. If you
are confident, make a nest of a folded tea towel and hold
the oyster in your other hand, otherwise hold it firmly
down on the board. Insert the point of the knife between
the two parts of the shell at the slightly narrower end.
Cut through the muscle and the flat top shell will come
away. Clean out any fragments of shell, making sure you
do not spill any of the liquid. Carefully cut the oyster to
loosen it from the bottom shell.

Whisk the oil, vinegar, salt and pepper together and add
the chopped shallots. Serve the oysters with a teaspoonful
or two of the shallot vinaigrette on top.

Brochetas de ahumado con fruta

Smoked fish and fruit brochettes

Makes 12

200 g (7 oz) smoked salmon
200 g (7 oz) smoked trout
200 g (7 oz) smoked mackerel
6 cherry tomatoes, halved
12 mixed green and red grapes, halved and deseeded
2 kiwi fruit, peeled and cut into 2-cm (¾-in) pieces
250 g (9 oz) assorted berries
(strawberries, raspberries, etc.)
6 green olives, pitted and halved
Freshly ground black pepper
1 lemon, quartered

Cut the fish into 3–4-cm (1½-in) pieces. Alternate pieces of the three fish, folding where necessary, with the cherry tomatoes, fruit and olives. Season lightly with pepper and squeeze over the juice from the lemon wedges.

Ceviche de gambas
Prawn ceviche

Makes about 20

700 g (1 lb 9 oz) fresh or frozen raw prawns (see note)
1 medium red onion, peeled and finely chopped
2 cloves garlic, peeled and crushed
Juice of 2 lemons or 2 Tbsp sherry vinegar
1 small bunch fresh parsley, finely chopped
Salt and freshly ground black pepper
100 ml (3½ fl oz) extra-virgin olive oil

Rinse the prawns and pat dry with kitchen paper. Shell
fresh prawns. Cut through the underside of each prawn,
devein and press flat to make a "butterfly". Lay the prawns
out in a wide, low dish and coat them with the mixture of
the onion, garlic, lemon juice or sherry vinegar, parsley,
salt and pepper. Cover and leave to marinate overnight.
An hour before serving, drain off the marinade and pour
on the olive oil. Thread on to skewers and serve.

Note: Soak thawed prawns for about 30 minutes in 500 ml
(18 fl oz) very cold water in which 2 tablespoons of sea salt
have been dissolved. This will refresh them and firm up the
flesh.

Gambas al ajillo
Garlic prawns

Serves 6

125 ml (4 fl oz) light olive oil
6 cloves garlic, peeled and chopped
1 small chilli, chopped
12 large prawns (tiger or king) or 350 g (12½ oz) peeled
raw prawns
2 tsp paprika
Sea salt
2 Tbsp chopped parsley
Juice of ½ lemon

Heat the oil to 180°C (350°F) in a large, heavy-bottomed frying pan, if you do not have earthenware cazuelitas.

Add the garlic and chilli to the oil, fry for 1 minute, then add the prawns and paprika. Season with salt and cook for a further 5 minutes. If the prawns are shelled, cook for only 2 to 3 minutes. When the prawns start to sizzle, add the parsley, squeeze over the lemon juice and serve immediately.

Note: Authentic presentation demands the prawns be cooked, and then brought sizzling to the table, in individual, heatproof earthenware bowls, called cazuelitas. They are most often served in their shells, but can be shelled first and then served on cocktail sticks.

Anchoas con pate de olivas

Toast with anchovies and black olive paste

Makes 12

1 French stick, cut into 1-cm (½-in) rounds
2 Tbsp good-quality olive oil
2 Tbsp tapenade (black olive paste)
12–24 marinated anchovies (boquerones, see page 21)
1 Tbsp extra-virgin olive oil
3 Tbsp vinegreta

Preheat the oven to 190°C (375°F/Gas Mark 5). Brush a little olive oil onto the bread, place on a baking tray and bake for 5 minutes or until golden brown.

Spread the toasted bread slices with a little tapenade. Remove the anchovies from their marinade and drizzle with the olive oil. Place one or two anchovies, depending on their size, onto each toasted bread slice. Add a little more tapenade and drizzle over a little vinagreta.

Vegetables

Exciting vegetable dishes that can be served on their own or alongside other tapas.

Champiñones rellenos
Stuffed mushrooms

Serves 6

15 large button mushrooms
3 shallots, peeled and very finely chopped
1 Tbsp light olive oil or 25 g (1 oz) butter
Salt and freshly ground black pepper
Pinch of grated nutmeg
50 g (2 oz) soft breadcrumbs
1 Tbsp parsley, finely chopped
1 Tbsp Parmesan or Manchego, finely grated (optional)
1 egg, beaten

Preheat the oven to 200°C (400°F/Gas Mark 6). Wipe the mushrooms clean and remove the stalks. Chop the stalks and the shallots very finely.

Heat the oil or butter in a medium frying pan to high. Add the shallots and the stalks. Season well, adding the nutmeg. Toss over the heat for a further 3 to 4 minutes, then transfer the mixture to a bowl with a slatted spoon and add the breadcrumbs, parsley, cheese, if using, and finally the beaten egg. Mix thoroughly.

Stuff the mushroom caps with this mixture. Place the stuffed mushrooms on a baking tray, drizzle with the oil from the frying pan and bake in the oven for 5 to 7 minutes or until the mushroom caps have wilted slightly. Serve on cocktail sticks.

Patatas bravas
Fiery potatoes

Serves 10

1 Tbsp oil
1 medium onion, diced
½ bay leaf
1 guindilla chilli
1 Tbsp flour
1 tsp hot smoked paprika
Pimentón picante (hot paprika)
100 ml (3½ fl oz) water
1.5 kg (3 lb 5 oz) Maris Piper potatoes, peeled
2 cloves garlic, peeled and crushed
Salt
Oil for frying

Heat the oil in a frying pan. Add the onion and soften over a medium heat for a couple of minutes before adding the bay leaf and guindilla chilli. Cook for a further 2 to 3 minutes then sprinkle on the flour and, stirring continuously, add the paprika. Slowly add small amounts of the water, stirring continuously, until the sauce has the consistency of runny custard. Allow to simmer very gently for 10 minutes. Pass the sauce through a sieve and return to the heat.

If you are roasting the potatoes, preheat the oven to 230°C (450°F/Gas Mark 8). Cut the potatoes into small chunks and place in a lightly oiled roasting tin. Mix in the garlic, sprinkle with salt and roast for 20 minutes or until crisp and golden. To fry, cut the potatoes into thick-ish chips or ½-cm (¼-in) slices and mix in the garlic. Season with salt. Heat the oil in a large frying pan and fry the potatoes gently until soft, increasing the heat at the end to turn them golden. Drain. Coat the roasted or fried potatoes generously with the sauce and serve immediately.

Vinagreta
Oil and vinegar dressing

200 ml (7 fl oz) olive oil
60 ml (2 fl oz) red wine vinegar
Salt and freshly ground black pepper
1 Tbsp finely diced onion
1 Tbsp finely diced green onion
2 tsp finely diced guindilla chili
2 Tbsp finely chopped parsley
2 Tbsp finely diced pimientos de piquillo (see page 23)

Whisk together the oil and vinegar in a bowl and season
to taste. Whisk in any of the suggested additions,
according to your preference. Do remember to keep
the dice very fine.

Papas arrugadas con mojo picante

Wrinkled potatoes with fiery sauce

Serves 8–10

1 kg (2 lb 3 oz) salad or new potatoes
25 g (1 oz) coarse sea salt
4 cloves garlic, peeled and minced
Salt and freshly ground black pepper
1 tsp hot paprika
3 shallots, peeled and finely chopped
1 chilli, finely chopped
1 small green pepper, finely chopped
1 pinch chopped thyme
1 Tbsp good-quality olive oil
4 Tbsp white wine vinegar

Barely cover the potatoes with water in a large saucepan and simmer them gently until the water has evaporated. Just before it does, add the sea salt. The potato skins will wrinkle to form a salty crust – *papas arrugadas*.

Season the minced garlic with salt to form a paste, then add the pepper, paprika, shallots, chilli, green pepper, thyme, oil and the vinegar. Warm water is sometimes added to thin the sauce to taste. The traditional way to eat these is as finger food, dipping the potatoes into the sauce.

Ensaladilla rusa
Russian salad

Serves 8–10

1 French stick, cut into 1-cm (½-in) rounds
6 large potatoes, unpeeled
1 large carrot, peeled and diced
115 g (4 oz) green beans, halved
115 g (4 oz) frozen petits pois
3 hard-boiled eggs, cut into eighths
1 large red pepper, deseeded and diced
3 guindillas, chopped (see page 21)
12 salted black olives
425 ml (¾ pint) mayonnaise

Toast the bread if you wish. In a large saucepan of salted water, simmer the potatoes whole for up to 30 minutes or until they are done. When they are cool enough to handle, peel and cut into 1-cm (½-in) cubes.

Drop the diced carrot into boiling salted water, bring back to the boil and simmer for a couple of minutes before adding the green beans and frozen peas. Bring back to the boil, simmer for another minute then drain, refreshing under cold, running water.

Mix together all the ingredients (though not the bread!) in a large bowl. Heap a large spoonful onto each round and serve.

Broccoli picante
Spicy broccoli

Serves 8–10

450 g (1 lb) broccoli florets
Salt
2 Tbsp good-quality olive oil
2 cloves garlic, peeled and minced
2 chillis, finely chopped
1 Tbsp toasted sesame seeds

Bring to the boil just enough salted water to cover the broccoli, turn down the heat, then simmer for no longer than 90 seconds – the broccoli must be crunchy! Drain immediately and refresh under cold running water. Drain thoroughly again.

Heat the oil in a large frying pan and add the garlic and chillis. Add the broccoli and coat well with the oil then sprinkle with the sesame seeds. Serve on cocktail sticks.

Coliflor rebozada
Cauliflower fritters

Makes about 24

For the batter:
150 ml (5 fl oz) milk
3 Tbsp white wine
3 Tbsp light olive oil
1 large egg, separated
1 tsp dry yeast
Salt
About 250 g (9 oz) plain flour

1 large cauliflower, cut into florets
350 ml (12 fl oz) oil for frying
2 lemons, quartered

Start by making the batter. Put the milk, wine, oil, egg yolk, yeast and a teaspoon of salt into a bowl. Stir well with a wooden spoon and add the flour, little by little, stirring continuously until you achieve a batter the consistency of single cream. You may need less flour. Set aside in a warm place to rest for half an hour.

Trim the stalks of the cauliflower florets and place in a large pan of boiling salted water. Bring back to the boil and simmer for 2 to 3 minutes – they should not be overcooked. Drain and refresh in cold water, then set out to dry on a tea towel.

Heat the oil to 180°C (350°F) in a large, wide pan suitable for deep-frying. Whisk the egg white to a stiff peak and fold it into the batter. This must be done at the last moment. One by one, coat the florets in the batter and drop into the oil to deep-fry in batches of no more than five. When golden, remove with a slotted spoon and drain on kitchen paper. Keep warm while you fry the rest. Squeeze over the juice from the lemon wedges and serve immediately.

Garbanzos con espinacas
Chickpeas with spinach

Serves 6

3 Tbsp good-quality olive oil
1 large slice of bread
750 g (1 lb 10 oz) fresh spinach leaves
240-g (7½-oz) tin of chickpeas, drained and rinsed
2 cloves garlic, peeled and minced
Salt and freshly ground black pepper
1 tsp ground cumin, ground
1 tsp paprika
2 Tbsp water
1 Tbsp wine vinegar

Heat 1 tablespoon of the oil in a large frying pan and fry the bread until golden. Remove and reserve.

Rinse the spinach thoroughly and shake off most of the water. In a large saucepan, heat the spinach until it wilts, tossing or stirring it repeatedly. Drain thoroughly, squeezing out the excess water with a wooden spoon and coarsely chop the spinach.

Add the rest of the oil to the pan, then the spinach and warm through before stirring in the chickpeas and garlic. Season well and add the cumin and paprika. Finely crumble the fried bread and stir into the mixture. Add the water and vinegar, stir and simmer gently for a couple of minutes. Serve in ramekins.

Aceitunas aliñadas
Marinated olives

Makes one 850-ml (1½-pint) jar

450 g (1 lb) large, brined olives, green or black
Selection of fresh herbs, to include 2 bay leaves, thyme,
rosemary and oregano
12 mixed peppercorns
2 small chillis, chopped
290 ml (½ pint) light olive oil
1 lemon, cut into eighths

Soak the olives in warm water for a few minutes then
rinse. Drain and pat them dry. In a bowl, mix all the dry
ingredients together before adding the oil and mixing
again. Pack the olives into a large, lidded jar with the
lemon wedges and pour over all the oil then firmly screw
on the lid. For best results, store them for several days –
the longer the better – turning every other day. These will
keep for several weeks in the fridge.

Tartaletas con pisto manchego
Ratatouille tartlets

Makes 12 tartlets

250 g (9 oz) ready-made puff pastry
Flour for dusting
3 Tbsp light olive oil
2 large Spanish onions, peeled, halved and finely sliced
3 large peppers (red, green and yellow),
deseeded and cut into strips
3 cloves garlic, peeled and minced
6 large, very ripe tomatoes, skinned, deseeded and
chopped or two 400-g (14-oz) tins peeled plum tomatoes
3 large courgettes, cut into ½ cm (¼ in) rounds
Salt and freshly ground black pepper
2 Tbsp parsley, chopped

Preheat the oven to 190°C (375°F/Gas Mark 5). Roll out
the pastry on a floured board and use it to line 12 tartlet
moulds. Place in the oven and cook for about 5 minutes or
until the pastry turns golden and starts to puff up. Remove
from the oven and keep warm.

Heat the oil in a large frying pan, add the onions, then after
5 minutes, the peppers. These should soften thoroughly, for
at least 15 minutes. Stir in the garlic and tomatoes and cook
for a further 10 minutes. Now add the courgettes and stew
for 10 more minutes. Season well, then stir in the parsley.
Heap onto the warm pastry tartlets and serve.

Calabazines en tomate
Courgettes in tomato sauce

Serves 8–10

1 kg (2 lb 3 oz) courgettes, cut into 1-cm (½-in) rounds
2 Tbsp light olive oil
2 cloves garlic, peeled and minced
320-g (11½-oz) jar best quality tomato sauce
Salt and freshly ground black pepper
1 tsp paprika (optional)

Heat a large, heavy-bottomed, preferably ridged griddle pan. When very hot, arrange the courgette rounds in it and allow to char slightly, for 3 to 4 minutes. Turn and grill the other side for a further 3 to 4 minutes. Remove the rounds from the pan and set aside. Repeat with the next batch.

Heat a large pan and soften the garlic in the oil. Add the tomato sauce and reduce slightly, for about 5 minutes – you want the sauce to be thick enough to coat the courgettes, not have them swimming in it. Season and add the paprika, if using. Add the grilled courgettes to the pan and stir thoroughly to coat. Serve a couple of the rounds on a cocktail stick.

Gazpacho rojo
Red gazpacho

Serves 10, as a tapa

75 g (2½ oz) white breadcrumbs or stale bread
4 Tbsp good olive oil
2 cloves garlic, peeled and minced
1 tsp salt
500 g (1 lb 2 oz) passata (creamed and sieved tomatoes)
or 225 g (8 oz) tinned tomatoes
4 pimientos de piquillo (see page 23)
1 small cucumber, diced
Juice of 1 lemon
1 Tbsp red wine vinegar
Iced water

In a bowl, blend the breadcrumbs with the oil. If using stale
bread, soak it in water and squeeze out the excess liquid.
Place all the ingredients, except for the water, in a blender
and purée until you achieve a very smooth paste.

At this point, you have the base for the soup. You need
only to add water to the blender to reach the consistency
required. Some people add almost no water, while others
prefer a much thinner soup. Serve in small coffee cups.

Ensalada andaluza en brocheta
Brochettes of Andalucian salad

Makes 8–10 brochettes

2 large sweet Spanish onions
2 medium aubergines
3 medium courgettes
2 large red peppers
4 beef tomatoes
10 cloves garlic, only 2 peeled and minced
4 Tbsp good-quality olive oil
2 Tbsp white wine vinegar
Salt and freshly ground black pepper
1 tsp cumin
2 Tbsp finely chopped parsley

Preheat the oven to 180°C (350°F/Gas Mark 4). Place the whole onions (unpeeled), aubergines and courgettes on a large baking tray and roast for about 20 minutes. Add the whole peppers and return to the oven for another 10 minutes. Then add the whole tomatoes and 8 unpeeled garlic cloves. Prick the aubergine with a fork and return the tray to the oven for a further 15 minutes. The timing can vary, depending on the size of the vegetables. Those which appear soft and ready can be removed earlier.

Place the peppers into a plastic bag for 10 minutes, then rub off the skin. Peel the onions and roasted garlic cloves. Cut the aubergines and courgettes into 2-cm (¾-in) cubes, the peppers and onions into similar-size triangles, and the tomatoes into halves and then quarters. Place all these ingredients in a large bowl.

To make the dressing, mix the 2 remaining garlic cloves into the oil and vinegar and season, then add the cumin and parsley. Thread the vegetables onto skewers and pour over the dressing. Allow to marinate for a few minutes before serving.

Almendras tostadas
Salted almonds

Serves 4–6

250 g (9 oz) shelled raw almonds
1–2 tsp sea salt

Preheat the oven to 220°C (400°F/Gas Mark 6). Place the almonds in a bowl and generously sprinkle them with water. Toss them to ensure they are all coated and a little damp. Add the salt – the quantity really is a matter of taste and, of course, you can leave the salt out altogether. Spread the almonds out evenly on a baking tray.

Roast the almonds for about 15 minutes, shaking them once or twice. This will dry them out, leaving the skins coated with the salt. If you like the almonds highly roasted, leave them in for up to another 10 minutes. Be careful not to allow them to burn, which can happen in the blink of an eye.

Champiñones al ajillo
Garlic mushrooms

Serves 6–8

2 Tbsp light olive oil or 50 g (2 oz) butter
450 g (1 lb) closed cup mushrooms
Salt and freshly ground black pepper
4 cloves garlic, peeled and minced
1 Tbsp parsley, finely chopped
Juice of ½ lemon

Heat the oil or butter in a very large frying pan. Add the whole mushrooms and fry gently for 10 minutes or so. Cover for the first couple of minutes, then stir occasionally to assist the steaming process.

Turn up the heat, season well and add the garlic. Continue to stir and cook until most of the liquid has evaporated and the mushrooms are no longer steaming, for another 5 or so minutes. Finally, sprinkle on the parsley and lemon juice, then stir through. Thread a couple of mushrooms on each cocktail stick and serve warm.

Ajo blanco con uvas
Almond soup with grapes

Serves 10, as a tapa

110 g (4 oz) blanched almonds
165 g (6 oz) soft white breadcrumbs
3 Tbsp good-quality olive oil
2 Tbsp white wine vinegar
2 cloves garlic, peeled and minced
1 tsp salt
Iced water
10 muscat grapes, deseeded and halved

Whizz the almonds in the blender, gradually adding the breadcrumbs, oil, vinegar, garlic and salt. This forms the base of the soup. Now gradually add enough water to achieve the consistency you like, about 250–450 ml (9–16 fl oz). Correct the seasoning to taste. Chill the soup for several hours and serve in small coffee cups, putting a grape in each cup.

Cocarrois
Spinach and raisin tartlets

Makes 12 tartlets

225 g (8 oz) ready-made puff pastry
Flour for dusting
75 g (2½ oz) raisins
1 kg (2 lb 3 oz) fresh spinach leaves
1 Tbsp light olive oil
50 g (2 oz) pine nuts
1 clove garlic, peeled and minced
Salt and freshly ground black pepper
1 tsp sweet paprika

Preheat the oven to 190°C (375°F/Gas Mark 5). Roll the pastry out onto a floured board and use to line 12 tartlet moulds. Place in the oven and bake for about 5 minutes or until the pastry turns golden. Remove from the oven and keep warm.

In a bowl, pour boiling water over the raisins and allow to soften for at least 15 minutes, then drain. If using muscatel raisins, deseed them now. Rinse the spinach thoroughly and shake off most of the water. In a large saucepan, heat the spinach until it wilts, tossing or stirring it repeatedly. Drain thoroughly, squeezing out the excess water with a wooden spoon. Coarsely chop the spinach and raisins together.

Heat the oil in a large frying pan, add the pine nuts and garlic and fry until they take a little colour. Stir in the chopped spinach and raisins, season well, add the paprika and cook through for another 5 minutes. Heap spoonsful of the spinach mixture into the tartlets and serve warm.

Calabazines con balsamico
Mediterranean courgettes

Serves 8–10

450 g (1 lb) courgettes, cut into 1-cm (½-in) rounds
2 Tbsp good-quality olive oil
1 Tbsp balsamic vinegar
Salt and freshly ground black pepper
Pinch of thyme
Pinch of oregano

Heat a large, heavy-bottomed, preferably ridged griddle pan. When very hot, arrange the courgette rounds in it and allow to char slightly, for 3 to 4 minutes. Turn and grill the other side for a further 3 to 4 minutes. Remove the rounds from the pan and place them in a bowl. Repeat with the next batch.

Add the remaining ingredients to the bowl and mix thoroughly. This is to be done while the courgettes are still warm. Add the second batch of the courgettes when done and mix again. Serve a couple of the coated courgette rounds on a cocktail stick.

Patatas pobres
Poor man's potatoes

Serves 8–10

450 g (1 lb) salad or new potatoes
2 Tbsp light olive oil
1 Spanish onion, peeled
3 peppers (red, green, yellow)
Salt and freshly ground black pepper
1 tsp mixed Mediterranean herbs
(rosemary, oregano, thyme etc)

Scrub the potatoes clean, put them in a large saucepan of cold, salted water and bring gently to the boil. Simmer for 15 minutes or until they are cooked through. Remove from the heat, drain and set aside.

Heat the oil in a large frying pan. Cut the onion and the cored, deseeded peppers into 2-cm (¾-in) triangles. Soften the onion and peppers in the oil for a few minutes. Cut the potatoes into 2-cm (¾-in) thick rounds. Add to the pan and heat through for a few minutes, stirring carefully so as not to break them up. Season and add the herbs. Thread the potatoes and peppers alternately on cocktail sticks and serve.

Endibias al cabrales
Chicory with blue cheese cream sauce

Serves 10

10 heads of chicory, as small as possible
25 g (1 oz) butter
200 ml (7 fl oz) cream or soured cream
50 g (2 oz) Cabrales or Roquefort or any equivalent
blue cheese, crumbled
Salt and freshly ground black pepper

Put the endive into a saucepan of boiling salted water.
Bring back to the boil, lower the heat and simmer for 8 to
10 minutes. Drain well and squeeze out any excess water.

Cut the endives lengthways, ensuring the core is intact
to keep the leaves together. In a medium frying pan, melt
the butter and pour in the cream, turning up the heat
to simmer for 3 to 4 minutes. Add the cheese, stirring
continuously. Season well and cook for a few more
minutes until the sauce is quite thick. Return the endives
to the pan, stirring thoroughly so that they are all coated.
Remove from the heat and allow to cool until the sauce
has thickened. Serve each coated endive on a cocktail stick.

Index

189

Acknowledgements

The publisher would like to thank Denby
(www.denbypottery.co.uk) for supplying
glasses and tableware for photography.